NATURE
POEMS TO
INSPIRE

INTRODUCTION

Cherished by all cultures throughout history, gardens and the natural environment still continue to provide a source of wonder, solace, relaxation and give cause for positive reflection.

In this inspiring collection of poems and extracts we can see how poets over a period of almost 500 years have recorded their observations and enjoyment in the flora and fauna of the wildest and also the most highly managed forms of nature. They pay heartfelt homage to our climate, changing seasons, agricultural practices and the regional differences in our beautiful landscape.

A RED, RED ROSE

Robert Burns

Oh my love is like a red, red rose
   That's newly sprung in June:
My love is like the melody
   That's sweetly played in tune.

As fair art thou, my bonnie lass,
   So deep in love am I:
And I will love thee still, my dear,
   Till a' the seas gang dry.

Till a' the seas gang dry, my dear,
   And the rocks melt wi' the sun:
And I will love thee still, my dear,
   While the sands o' life shall run.

And fare thee weel, my only love,
   And fare thee weel a while!
And I will come again, my love,
   Tho' it were ten thousand mile.

THE WAY THROUGH THE WOODS

Rudyard Kipling

They shut the road through the woods
Seventy years ago.
Weather and rain have undone it again,
And now you would never know
There was once a road through the woods
Before they planted the trees.
It is underneath the coppice and heath,
And the thin anemones.
Only the keeper sees
That, where the ring-dove broods,
And the badgers roll at ease,
There was once a road through the woods.

Yet, if you enter the woods
Of a summer evening late,
When the night-air cools on the trout-ringed pools
Where the otter whistles his mate,
(They fear not men in the woods,
Because they see so few)
You will hear the beat of a horse's feet
And the swish of a skirt in the dew,
Steadily cantering through
The misty solitudes,
As though they perfectly knew
The old lost road through the woods.
But there is no road through the woods.

THE FLOWER

Alfred Tennyson

Once in a golden hour
  I cast to earth a seed.
Up there came a flower,
  The people said, a weed.

To and fro they went
  Thro' my garden-bower,
And muttering discontent
  Curs'd me and my flower.

Then it grew so tall
  It wore a crown of light,
But thieves from o'er the wall
  Stole the seed by night.

Sow'd it far and wide
  By every town and tower,
Till all the people cried,
  "Splendid is the flower."

Read my little fable:
  He that runs may read.
Most can raise the flowers now,
  For all have got the seed.

And some are pretty enough,
  And some are poor indeed;
And now again the people
  Call it but a weed.

DAFFODILS

William Wordsworth

I wandered lonely as a cloud
      That floats on high o'er vales and hills,
When all at once I saw a crowd,
      A host, of golden daffodils;
Beside the lake, beneath the trees,
Fluttering and dancing in the breeze.

Continuous as the stars that shine
      And twinkle on the Milky Way,
They stretched in never-ending line
      Along the margin of a bay:
Ten thousand saw I at a glance,
Tossing their heads in sprightly dance.

The waves beside them danced, but they
      Out-did the sparkling waves in glee:
A poet could not but be gay,
      In such a jocund company:
I gazed – and gazed – but little thought
What wealth the show to me had brought:

For oft, when on my couch I lie
      In vacant or in pensive mood,
They flash upon that inward eye
      Which is the bliss of solitude;
And then my heart with pleasure fills,
And dances with the daffodils.

SONNET 98

William Shakespeare

From you have I been absent in the spring,
When proud-pied April dress'd in all his trim
Hath put a spirit of youth in every thing,
That heavy Saturn laugh'd and leap'd with him.
Yet nor the lays of birds nor the sweet smell
Of different flowers in odour and in hue
Could make me any summer's story tell,
Or from their proud lap pluck them where they grew;
Nor did I wonder at the lily's white,
Nor praise the deep vermilion in the rose;
They were but sweet, but figures of delight,
Drawn after you, you pattern of all those.
    Yet seem'd it winter still, and, you away,
    As with your shadow I with these did play.

LEISURE

William Henry Davies

What is this life if, full of care,
We have no time to stand and stare?

No time to stand beneath the boughs
And stare as long as sheep or cows:

No time to see, when woods we pass,
Where squirrels hide their nuts in grass:

No time to see, in broad daylight,
Streams full of stars like skies at night:

No time to turn at Beauty's glance,
And watch her feet, how they can dance:

No time to wait till her mouth can
Enrich that smile her eyes began?

A poor life this if, full of care,
We have no time to stand and stare.

——

THERE IS ANOTHER SKY

——

Emily Dickinson

There is another sky,
Ever serene and fair,
And there is another sunshine,
Though it be darkness there;
Never mind faded forests, Austin,
Never mind silent fields –
Here is a little forest,
Whose leaf is ever green;
Here is a brighter garden,
Where not a frost has been;
In its unfading flowers
I hear the bright bee hum:
Prithee, my brother,
Into my garden come!

THE LAKE ISLE OF INNISFREE

William Butler Yeats

I will arise and go now, and go to Innisfree,
And a small cabin build there, of clay and wattles made:
Nine bean-rows will I have there, a hive for the honey-bee,
And live alone in the bee-loud glade.

And I shall have some peace there, for peace comes dropping slow,
Dropping from the veils of the morning to where the cricket sings;
There midnight's all a glimmer, and noon a purple glow,
And evening full of the linnet's wings.

I will arise and go now, for always night and day
I hear lake water lapping with low sounds by the shore;
While I stand on the roadway, or on the pavements grey,
I hear it in the deep heart's core.

FROM ODE TO A NIGHTINGALE

John Keats

My heart aches, and a drowsy numbness pains
     My sense, as though of hemlock I had drunk,
Or emptied some dull opiate to the drains
     One minute past, and Lethe-wards had sunk:
'Tis not through envy of thy happy lot,
     But being too happy in thy happiness,
     That thou, light-wingèd Dryad of the trees,
        In some melodious plot
     Of beechen green, and shadows numberless,
     Singest of summer in full-throated ease.

II
O for a draught of vintage! that hath been
     Cooled a long age in the deep-delvèd earth,
Tasting of Flora and the country green,
     Dance, and Provençal song, and sunburnt mirth!
O for a beaker full of the warm South!
     Full of the true, the blushful Hippocrene,
     With beaded bubbles winking at the brim,
        And purple-stainèd mouth;
     That I might drink, and leave the world unseen,
     And with thee fade away into the forest dim.

—

FROM ELEGY WRITTEN IN A COUNTRY CHURCHYARD

—

Thomas Gray

The curfew tolls the knell of parting day,
The lowing herd wind slowly o'er the lea,
The ploughman homeward plods his weary way,
And leaves the world to darkness and to me.

Now fades the glimmering landscape on the sight,
And all the air a solemn stillness holds,
Save where the beetle wheels his droning flight,
And drowsy tinklings lull the distant folds;

Save that from yonder ivy-mantled tower
The moping owl does to the moon complain
Of such as, wandering near her secret bower,
Molest her ancient solitary reign.

Beneath those rugged elms, that yew-tree's shade,
Where heaves the turf in many a mouldering heap,
Each in his narrow cell for ever laid,
The rude forefathers of the hamlet sleep.

HOME THOUGHTS FROM ABROAD

Robert Browning

Oh, to be in England
Now that April's there,
And whoever wakes in England
Sees, some morning, unaware,
That the lowest boughs and the brushwood sheaf
Round the elm-tree bole are in tiny leaf,
While the chaffinch sings on the orchard bough
In England – now!

And after April, when May follows,
And the whitethroat builds, and all the swallows!
Hark, where my blossomed pear-tree in the hedge
Leans to the field and scatters on the clover
Blossoms and dewdrops – at the bent spray's edge –
That's the wise thrush; he sings each song twice over,
Lest you should think he never could recapture
The first fine careless rapture!
And though the fields look rough with hoary dew
All will be gay when noontide wakes anew
The buttercups, the little children's dower
– Far brighter than this gaudy melon-flower!

TO AUTUMN

John Keats

Season of mists and mellow fruitfulness!
      Close bosom-friend of the maturing sun;
Conspiring with him how to load and bless
      With fruit the vines that round the thatch-eaves run;
To bend with apples the mossed cottage-trees,
      And fill all fruit with ripeness to the core;
      To swell the gourd, and plump the hazel shells
With a sweet kernel; to set budding more,
      And still more, later flowers for the bees,
      Until they think warm days will never cease,
      For Summer has o'erbrimmed their clammy cells.

Who hath not seen thee oft amid thy store?
      Sometimes whoever seeks abroad may find
Thee sitting careless on a granary floor,
      Thy hair soft-lifted by the winnowing wind,
Or on a half-reaped furrow sound asleep,
      Drowsed with the fume of poppies, while thy hook
      Spares the next swath and all its twinèd flowers;
And sometimes like a gleaner thou dost keep
      Steady thy laden head across a brook;
      Or by a cider-press, with patient look,
      Thou watchest the last oozings hours by hours.

Where are the songs of Spring? Ay, where are they?
      Think not of them, thou hast thy music too, –
While barred clouds bloom the soft-dying day,
      And touch the stubble-plains with rosy hue;
Then in a wailful choir the small gnats mourn
      Among the river sallows, borne aloft
      Or sinking as the light wind lives or dies;
And full-grown lambs loud bleat from hilly bourn;
      Hedge-crickets sing; and now with treble soft
      The redbreast whistles from a garden-croft;
      And gathering swallows twitter in the skies.

———

IN FLANDERS FIELDS

———

John McCrae

In Flanders fields the poppies blow
Between the crosses, row on row,
      That mark our place; and in the sky
      The larks, still bravely singing, fly
Scarce heard amid the guns below.

We are the Dead. Short days ago
We lived, felt dawn, saw sunset glow,
      Loved and were loved, and now we lie
      In Flanders fields.

Take up our quarrel with the foe:
To you from failing hands we throw
      The torch; be yours to hold it high.
      If ye break faith with us who die
We shall not sleep, though poppies grow
      In Flanders fields.

LOVELIEST OF TREES

Alfred Edward Housman

Loveliest of trees, the cherry now
Is hung with bloom along the bough,
And stands about the woodland ride
Wearing white for Eastertide.

Now, of my threescore years and ten,
Twenty will not come again,
And take from seventy springs a score,
It only leaves me fifty more.

And since to look at things in bloom
Fifty springs are little room,
About the woodlands I will go
To see the cherry hung with snow.

—

ANSWER TO A CHILD'S QUESTION

—

Samuel Taylor Coleridge

Do you ask what the birds say? The Sparrow, the Dove,
The Linnet and Thrush say, 'I love and I love!'
In the winter they're silent – the wind is so strong;
What it says, I don't know, but it sings a loud song.
But green leaves, and blossoms, and sunny warm weather,
And singing, and loving – all come back together.
But the Lark is so brimful of gladness and love,
The green fields below him, the blue sky above,
That he sings, and he sings; and for ever sings he –
'I love my Love, and my Love loves me!'

ENGLAND

Walter de la Mare

No lovelier hills than thine have laid
    My tired thoughts to rest;
No peace of lovelier valleys made
    Like peace within my breast.

Thine are the woods whereto my soul,
    Out of the noontide beam,
Flees for a refuge green and cool
    And tranquil as a dream.

Thy breaking seas like trumpets peal;
    Thy clouds – how oft have I
Watched their bright towers of silence steal
    Into infinity!

My heart within me faints to roam
    In thought even far from thee:
Thine be the grave whereto I come,
    And thine my darkness be.

THE GLORY OF THE GARDEN

Rudyard Kipling

Our England is a garden that is full of stately views,
Of borders, beds and shrubberies and lawns and avenues,
With statues on the terraces and peacocks strutting by;
But the Glory of the Garden lies in more than meets the eye.
For where the old thick laurels grow, along the thin red wall,
You'll find the tool- and potting-sheds which are the heart of all;
The cold-frames and the hot-houses, the dung-pits and the tanks,
The rollers, carts, and drain-pipes, with the barrows and the planks.

And there you'll see the gardeners, the men and 'prentice boys
Told off to do as they are bid and do it without noise;
For, except when seeds are planted and we shout to scare the birds,
The Glory of the Garden it abideth not in words.
And some can pot begonias and some can bud a rose,
And some are hardly fit to trust with anything that grows;
But they can roll and trim the lawns and sift the sand and loam,
For the Glory of the Garden occupieth all who come.

Our England is a garden, and such gardens are not made
By singing:– 'Oh, how beautiful,' and sitting in the shade
While better men than we go out and start their working lives
At grubbing weeds from gravel-paths with broken dinner-knives.
There's not a pair of legs so thin, there's not a head so thick,
There's not a hand so weak and white, nor yet a heart so sick
But it can find some needful job that's crying to be done,
For the Glory of the Garden glorifieth every one.

Then seek your job with thankfulness and work till further orders,
If it's only netting strawberries or killing slugs on borders;
And when your back stops aching and your hands begin to harden,
You will find yourself a partner in the Glory of the Garden.
Oh, Adam was a gardener, and God who made him sees
That half a proper gardener's work is done upon his knees,
So when your work is finished, you can wash your hands and pray
For the Glory of the Garden that it may not pass away!

And the Glory of the Garden it shall never pass away!

YOUNG LAMBS

John Clare

The spring is coming by a many signs;
The trays are up, the hedges broken down,
That fenced the haystack, and the remnant shines
Like some old antique fragment weathered brown.
And where suns peep, in every sheltered place,
The little early buttercups unfold
A glittering star or two – till many trace
The edges of the blackthorn clumps in gold.
And then a little lamb bolts up behind
The hill and wags his tail to meet the yoe,
And then another, sheltered from the wind,
Lies all his length as dead – and lets me go
Close bye and never stirs but baking lies,
With legs stretched out as though he could not rise.

SPRING

Gerard Manley Hopkins

Nothing is so beautiful as Spring –
   When weeds, in wheels, shoot long and lovely and lush;
   Thrush's eggs look little low heavens, and thrush
Through the echoing timber does so rinse and wring
The ear, it strikes like lightnings to hear him sing;
   The glassy peartree leaves and blooms, they brush
   The descending blue; that blue is all in a rush
With richness; the racing lambs too have fair their fling.

What is all this juice and all this joy?
   A strain of the earth's sweet being in the beginning
In Eden garden. – Have, get, before it cloy,
   Before it cloud, Christ, lord, and sour with sinning,
Innocent mind and Mayday in girl and boy,
   Most, O maid's child, thy choice and worthy the winning.

—

THE HEREFORDSHIRE LANDSCAPE

—

FROM: AURORA LEIGH

Elizabeth Barrett Browning

I dared to rest, or wander, – like a rest
Made sweeter for the step upon the grass, –
And view the ground's most gentle dimplement,
(As if God's finger touched but did not press
In making England!) such an up and down
Of verdure, – nothing too much up or down,
A ripple of land; such little hills, the sky
Can stoop to tenderly and the wheatfields climb;
Such nooks of valleys, lined with orchises,
Fed full of noises by invisible streams;
And open pastures, where you scarcely tell
White daisies from white dew, – at intervals
The mythic oaks and elm-trees standing out
Self-poised upon their prodigy of shade ...

But then the thrushes sang,
And shook my pulses and the elms' new leaves...

I flattered all the beauteous country round,
As poets use; the skies, the clouds, the fields,
The happy violets hiding from the roads
The primroses run down to, carrying gold, –
The tangled hedgerows, where the cows push out
Impatient horns and tolerant churning mouths
'Twixt dripping ash-boughs, – hedgerows all alive
With birds and gnats and large white butterflies
Which look as if the May-flower had caught life
And palpitated forth upon the wind, –
Hills, vales, woods, netted in a silver mist,
Farms, granges, doubled up among the hills,
And cattle grazing in the watered vales,
And cottage-chimneys smoking from the woods,
And cottage-gardens smelling everywhere,
Confused with smell of orchards.

THE GARDEN

Andrew Marvell

How vainly men themselves amaze
To win the palm, the oak, or bays,
And their uncessant labours see
Crown'd from some single herb or tree,
Whose short and narrow verged shade
Does prudently their toils upbraid;
While all flow'rs and all trees do close
To weave the garlands of repose.

Fair Quiet, have I found thee here,
And Innocence, thy sister dear!
Mistaken long, I sought you then
In busy companies of men;
Your sacred plants, if here below,
Only among the plants will grow.
Society is all but rude,
To this delicious solitude.

No white nor red was ever seen
So am'rous as this lovely green.
Fond lovers, cruel as their flame,
Cut in these trees their mistress' name;
Little, alas, they know or heed
How far these beauties hers exceed!
Fair trees! wheres'e'er your barks I wound,
No name shall but your own be found.

When we have run our passion's heat,
Love hither makes his best retreat.
The gods, that mortal beauty chase,
Still in a tree did end their race:
Apollo hunted Daphne so,
Only that she might laurel grow;
And Pan did after Syrinx speed,
Not as a nymph, but for a reed.

What wond'rous life in this I lead!
Ripe apples drop about my head;
The luscious clusters of the vine
Upon my mouth do crush their wine;
The nectarine and curious peach
Into my hands themselves do reach;
Stumbling on melons as I pass,
Ensnar'd with flow'rs, I fall on grass.

Meanwhile the mind, from pleasure less,
Withdraws into its happiness;
The mind, that ocean where each kind
Does straight its own resemblance find,
Yet it creates, transcending these,
Far other worlds, and other seas;
Annihilating all that's made
To a green thought in a green shade.

Here at the fountain's sliding foot,
Or at some fruit tree's mossy root,
Casting the body's vest aside,
My soul into the boughs does glide;
There like a bird it sits and sings,
Then whets, and combs its silver wings;
And, till prepar'd for longer flight,
Waves in its plumes the various light.

Such was that happy garden-state,
While man there walk'd without a mate;
After a place so pure and sweet,
What other help could yet be meet!
But 'twas beyond a mortal's share
To wander solitary there:
Two paradises 'twere in one
To live in paradise alone.

How well the skillful gard'ner drew
Of flow'rs and herbs this dial new,
Where from above the milder sun
Does through a fragrant zodiac run;
And as it works, th' industrious bee
Computes its time as well as we.
How could such sweet and wholesome hours
Be reckon'd but with herbs and flow'rs!

THE GARDENER

Robert Louis Stevenson

The gardener does not love to talk.
He makes me keep the gravel walk;
And when he puts his tools away,
He locks the door and takes the key.

Away behind the currant row,
Where no one else but cook may go,
Far in the plots, I see him dig,
Old and serious, brown and big.

He digs the flowers, green, red, and blue,
Nor wishes to be spoken to.
He digs the flowers and cuts the hay,
And never seems to want to play.

Silly gardener! summer goes,
And winter comes with pinching toes,
When in the garden bare and brown
You must lay your barrow down.

Well now, and while the summer stays,
To profit by these garden days
O how much wiser you would be
To play at Indian wars with me!

THE LITTLE GARDEN

Amy Lowell

A little garden on a bleak hillside
Where deep the heavy, dazzling mountain snow
Lies far into the spring. The sun's pale glow
Is scarcely able to melt patches wide
About the single rose bush. All denied
Of nature's tender ministries. But no, –
For wonder-working faith has made it blow
With flowers many hued and starry-eyed.
Here sleeps the sun long, idle summer hours;
Here butterflies and bees fare far to rove
Amid the crumpled leaves of poppy flowers;
Here four o'clocks, to the passionate night above
Fling whiffs of perfume, like pale incense showers.
A little garden, loved with a great love!

This edition published in 2017 by Baker & Taylor Uk Ltd,
Bicester, Oxfordshire OX26 4ST

All Images reproduced courtesy of Shutterstock
except pages 60–61 © Jack Bailey / ardea.com

Cover design: Milestone Creative
Contents design: seagulls.net

ISBN 978-1-910562-89-5

'England' by Walter de la Mare reproduced courtesy of the Society of
Authors as the Literary Representatives of the Estate of Walter de la Mare

Printed in China by Wai Man Book Binding (China) ltd